Frogs

Marfé Ferguson Delano

NATIONAL
GEOGRAPHIC
KiDS

WASHINGTON, D.C.

Look, a frog!

Up in a tree, a tiny tree frog balances on a branch. Tree frogs tiptoe on twigs and leap onto leaves. Sticky toe tips help tree frogs climb and cling.

Down by a stream, a big bullfrog snuggles into squishy, mushy mud. *Squelch!*

In a sandy desert, a spadefoot toad digs with shovel-like back feet, burrowing underground.

Sploosh!

Out in a pond, a leggy leopard frog launches off a lily pad. It arches through the air and splashes into the water.

Home Sweet Home

Frogs live almost everywhere on Earth, except Antarctica. You can find them on mountaintops, in forests, creeks and rivers, ponds and lakes, fields, parks, gardens, and deserts.

Pacman frog
South America

spadefoot toad
North America

Australian green tree frog
Australia

Fleischmann's glass frog
Central America

There are more than 5,000 kinds of frogs. Here are some from around the world.

flaming
poison dart frog
Central and
South America

Wallace
flying frog
Southeast
Asia

Vietnamese
mossy frog
Southeast
Asia

Frogs come in many different colors and sizes. They can be tiny or they can be huge.

Frogs can be bumpy, or frogs can be smooth. Some frogs are even see-through!

Most mother frogs lay
eggs in or near water.

Pop!

When the eggs hatch, out pop tiny tadpoles. They live underwater and eat tiny plants. They look like fish, but they are wiggly, wriggly baby frogs, also known as pollywogs.

Tadpoles start
out with chubby,
stubby bodies and
long, flat tails.
But as a tadpole
grows, its body
changes. It sprouts
legs for swimming
and hopping.

Its tail gets smaller and smaller. Its eyes get bulgier and bulgier. Its mouth gets wider and wider.

Finally the tadpole looks like a frog. Out of the water it crawls.

Now the young frog is ready to explore its new world—and to eat!

Gulp!

This frog loves to eat bugs. It shoots out its sticky tongue to snap up a passing insect, pulls the prey into its mouth, and swallows it whole.

Froggy Feasts

How far can you stick out your tongue?

Frogs are *not* fussy eaters. They will eat just about anything that moves, as long as it can fit into their mouths.

Bugs and caterpillars are fine food for frogs!

Do you think a worm tastes yummy or yucky?

Frogs chow down on insects, spiders, worms, slugs, and snails. Some large frogs also dine on mice, and even other frogs!

How would you like lizards for lunch and spiders for supper?

This frog just nabbed a delicious dragonfly.

This mouse better watch out for big hungry frogs!

Frogs eat all kinds of animals, and all kinds of animals eat frogs!

Birds and bats, snakes and rats, raccoons, fish, lizards, crocodiles, and even bears all gobble up frogs.

How do frogs survive?
Some hide by blending
into the background.

Some have brilliant colors
that warn hungry hunters,
"Don't eat me!" These
brightly hued frogs have
poison in their skin.

Jump, frog!

A frog on the ground can leap to safety. And in a treetop, a gliding frog spreads its toes wide, jumps off a branch, and glides. Happy landing!

All in the Family

Moist, smooth skin. What does your skin feel like?

No tail

Bulging eyes. Can you make your eyes look really big?

Long, strong legs for jumping and leaping. Can you leap like a frog?

Teeth in upper jaw

Four toes on front

Don't let toads fool you. Despite their name, toads are a kind of frog. But that doesn't mean frogs and toads are exactly alike. Frogs live most of their lives around water. Toads can be found in drier places, even in deserts! Here are some ways that frogs and toads are different—and the same.

Poison gland behind each eye

Dry, bumpy skin. What other things feel bumpy?

No tail

No teeth

Short legs, just right for walking or short hops. Can you make short hops like a toad?

Four toes on front legs. How many fingers and toes do you have?

Five toes on hind legs

Toad

Sing Like a Frog!

Even when you can't see frogs, you can often hear them singing. Some frogs puff up their throats like balloons to make sound. Each type of frog has its own special call. Some are so loud they can be heard a mile away! Here are some frog calls. Can you make these froggy sounds?

bullfrog:
JUG-O-RUM

spring peeper:
PEEP PEEP PEEP

red-eyed tree frog: *CHOCK CHOCK CHOCK*

coqui frog: *CO-KEE!*

gray tree frog: *TRILLLLL*

wood frog: *QUACK QUACK QUACK*

For Bill Delano, a wonderful nephew and fellow frog facer
—MFD

Editors: Ariane Szu-Tu
Art Director: Amanda Larsen
Photography Editor: Lori Epstein

National Geographic supports K–12 educators with ELA Common Core Resources. Visit www.natgeoed.org/commoncore for more information.

Trade paperback ISBN: 978-1-4263-1697-5
Reinforced library binding ISBN: 978-1-4263-1698-2

The publisher gratefully acknowledges herpetologist Dr. Harold Voris of the Field Museum of Natural History and early education expert Dr. Alice Wilder for their expert review of the book.

ILLUSTRATIONS CREDITS

Cover, Gregory Basco/Visuals Unlimited, Inc./Getty Images; back cover, Eric Isselée/Shutterstock; 1, Mircea Bezergheanu/Shutterstock; 2-3, Hector Ruiz Villar/Shutterstock; 4–5, Michael Durham/Minden Pictures; 6, Gerry Ellis and Michael Durham/Digital Vision; 6 (Background), rachisan alexandra/Shutterstock; 7, Do Van Dijck/Foto Natura/Minden Pictures; 8, Bianca Lavies/National Geographic Creative; 9, Robert Pickett/Visuals Unlimited/Corbis; 10 (UP), kikkerdirk/iStockphoto; 10 (CTR), iliuta goean/Shutterstock; 10 (LOLE), George Grall/National Geographic Creative; 10 (LORT), Cathy Keifer/iStockphoto; 11 (UP), Stephen Dalton/Minden Pictures; 11 (CTR), Paul Zahl/National Geographic Creative; 11 (LO), Joe McDonald/Corbis; 12, Dirk Ercken/Shutterstock; 13 (UP), aida ricciardiello/Shutterstock; 13 (LO), J.P. Lawrence/Shutterstock; 13 (Background), xxttaa/Shutterstock; 14, George Grall/National Geographic Creative; 15, Alvin E Staffan/Photo Researchers RM/Getty Images; 16, Robert Clay/Ambient Images; 17 (UP), Dan Suzio/Photo Researchers RM/Getty Images; 17 (LO), Dan Suzio/Photo Researchers RM/Getty Images; 18, Stephen Dalton/Minden Pictures; 19, Buddy Mays/Corbis; 20 (UP), Oktay Ortakcioglu/Vetta/Getty Images; 20 (CTR), irin-k/Shutterstock; 20 (LOLE), Anest/Shutterstock; 20 (LORT), waysidelynne/Shutterstock; 21 (UP), Sascha Gebhardt/Shutterstock; 21 (CTR), S-F/Shutterstock; 21 (LORT), Gary Meszaros/Photo Researchers RM/Getty Images; 21 (LOLE), epantha/iStockphoto; 22, blickwinkel/Alamy; 23 (UP), Eduard Kyslynskyy/Shutterstock; 23 (LO), Jonathan Blair/Corbis; 24, Lorraine Hudgins/Shutterstock; 25, Dirk Ercken/Shutterstock; 26–27, Stephen Dalton/Minden Pictures; 28, Tsekhmister/Shutterstock; 29, Vitalii Hulai/Shutterstock; 30 (UP), Bruce MacQueen/Shutterstock; 30 (LO), Brian Lasenby/Shutterstock; 31 (UPLE), Wollertz/Shutterstock; 31 (UPRT), Dante Fenolio/Photo Researchers RM/Getty Images; 31 (LOLE), Ryan M. Bolton/Shutterstock; 31 (LORT), Steve Byland/Shutterstock; 32, Kitchin and Hurst/All Canada Photos/Getty Images

FROG NAMES BY PAGE NUMBER

Printed in the United States of America
14/WOR/1